MW00764043

Doctor Magdalena

Doctor Magdalena

Rosa Martha Villarreal

Novella

A TQS BOOK

TQS PUBLICATIONS
A Division of Tonatiuh-Quinto Sol International, Inc.
Post Office Box 9275 Berkeley, California 94709

First Printing: May 1995

Library of Congress Cataloging-in-Publication Data

Villarreal, Rosa Martha, 1955-
Doctor Magdalena : novella / Rosa Martha Villarreal.
p. cm.
ISBN 0-89229-031-5
I. Title.
PS3572.I373D63 1995
813' .54--dc20
95-12966
CIP

ISBN: 0-89229-031-5

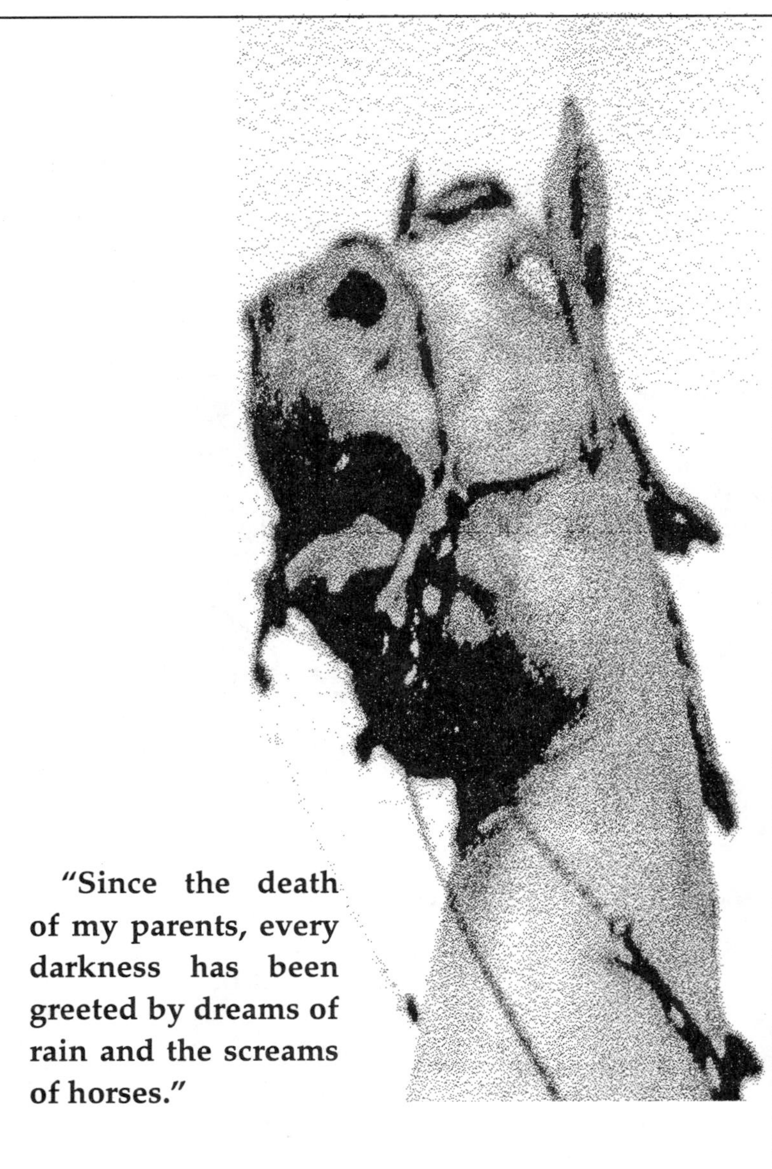

"Since the death of my parents, every darkness has been greeted by dreams of rain and the screams of horses."

Chapter One

Houston, Texas

Magdalena Ibarra:

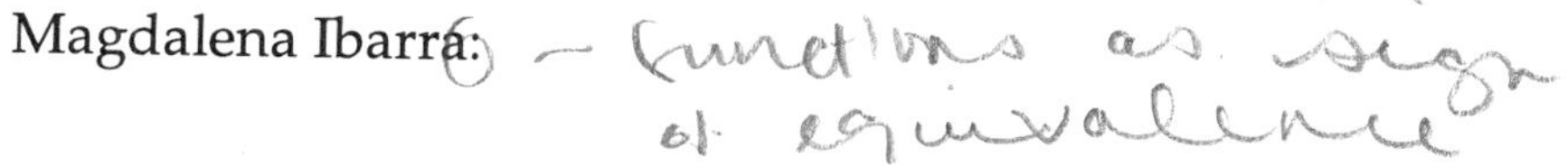

Since the death of my parents, every darkness has been greeted by dreams of rain and the screams of horses. With each darkness comes the cries of warriors consumed by the addiction of death, and I can hear the wails of women who are obsessed with the urge to regain the secret movements of the stars.

As the fire raged through their home, the death cries of my parents were carried by the trees until they reached me in my prison of reason. I am a woman of reason, a doctor, but the death of my parents unleashed my mind into a vortex of vertigo, that childhood illness of mine, a sight into a world buried in the caves of memory and the primal oceans of time, a swirling of colors and music of obscure tones. The night exiles me into the unseen world, a reality ridiculed as hallucination, or, perhaps, clinically classified as insanity.

The darkness arrives and again I am seized by that restlessness of memories. Sleep is a mere pretense. It is not rest. It is the haunting of my father's and mother's voices, screams in the fire, *"¡Magdalena, hija!"* They stalk me in this nightmare of pain as if I could save them, as if my childhood faith in them could save them from the pangs of conscience in the solitude of death. Doctor Rodolfo Ibarra and his wife, Doña Isabela, the servants and lords of nuestra gente.

"Your land of dreams, memories, and desires deferred," whispers the voice of my father, *"is the secret of our redemption, hija."*

The geography of my own imagination, once safely tucked away in my father's conventions, repressed in his imposed wisdom, has suddenly invaded me because he is dead, as if he alone could protect me from some secret discovery in my night wanderings, as if my own dreams were forbidden. My father, the keeper of the ancient secrets. With his death the false order dies.

Why am I still held hostage to the false memory of my father and mother? I knew the bitter truth all along: my father, the respected doctor, who, with his wife, opened a medical practice in Houston. *"To serve nuestra gente,"* they said. But it was the other way around. It was the people who served them well: being prisoners to the Spanish tongue, they would come to their countryman, my father, who exploited them with an enduring contempt for their poverty.

I keep their shame locked in my heart. Once I believed I could personally undo their sins, their arrogance. That is why I became a doctor, like my father, and why I worked for the poor. Still, I am haunted by the voices of whispered Spanish, and by the songs in tongues now locked within the sleep of the dead. I am a prisoner of the sorrow my father caused, of the faces of poverty turned away in defeat and want.

"En la noche, hija, you will find the ...."

I dream that a horseman emerges from the flames of my parents' house as it burns. I no longer fight this and the other dreams with drugs. I let them lead me to ...where? Perhaps insanity. Perhaps death.

The blanket of night covers the city, and again I am deceived: I think that I am dreaming, but this is not a dream. I know it is not. I am a reasonable woman. I know a hallucination from a dream. This is neither. No. I am there, again, in Mexico City. My eyes are open, I am spinning into another dimension. I watch the ceiling of my room as my phantom self walks down the old sector in a labyrinth of memories. I can smell the decay of the Aztec Mercado as it desperately struggles against the weight of the eternal oblivion which threatens to consume it. The voice of my father enters through my ears like a liquid.

"Even the soul of a place wishes immortality for itself," he says.

I no longer watch myself. I am no longer an observer recalling the past. I am there, with my father, in the old sector of Mexico City as we walk along the streets where the palaces of the Spanish nobility have been converted into boarding houses.

"In this place nothing is forgotten, hija. That is why we bring you here. In Houston and the United States, time devours itself. There is no respect or nostalgia. But here," he points to the streets around us as if they are enclosed in a capsule of gray, *"here is where time comes and piles itself upon another time. Nothing is forgotten.*

Whenever you begin to forget your padres, if ever the urge overtakes you after we are dead, you must return to the city, hija, and you must remember whose daughter you are."

"Yes, padre."

For the rest of the night I am here and there in this unreality of time, in this spell of night. I am where time and the material universe dissolve. As light divides itself into its true nature through a spectrum, so does the universe and time reveal many layers and alternate possibilities in the vertigo of this night.

Only the light of day can break these spells, and then I can be myself again. Then I can go to work, hear my name spoken without an impending meaning: *"Doctor Magdalena Ibarra."* In the light of day I can hide from this nocturnal intrusion.

But, even in the time of day, when I wear my mask of professionalism, I know what the night visions mean: My father's spirit calls me to the great city. If I won't go then, he will come for me again when the darkness arrives. I have always hated the darkness and its secrets.

In the light of day, even the foulest of us seems respectable. It is as if the day is like old age. The old are forgiven their sins because they are old. The day does the same. I wish I didn't have to remember the darkness. I wish that I could sleep like an innocent. When the night arrives again, I observe my self-imposed solitude, since I have remained unmarried, and once again in pensive silence I contemplate the inviting vial of drugs. Take one, Doctor Ibarra, and pretend you have no memory. Push them away, perhaps they will die of aloneness. Perhaps — they will....

I am transported through the corridors of memory and time. I feel transformed as a child, but my consciousness of a grown woman remains intact. There are the voices in my grandmother's house. It is night. In secret, I listen. The murmurs of the voices reveal an evil from which only my father can save me. I get up. Softly, I walk back towards the kitchen. I, too, am seduced by the darkness and wish to remain a shadow. A flower patterned curtain separates the kitchen from the hallway where I remain. I hear the voices.

My grandmother: *"Rogelio gave his daughter to the cantina owner to pay off his gambling debt."*

My father: *"That can't be, mamá. Rogelio said they were married in Dolores Hidalgo during the fiesta of the 16th."*

My grandmother: *"Don't be a fool, Rodolfo . . . ."*

My father, brusquely interrupting: *"Mother, I am not a child. You cannot address me as a fool."*

His voice is full of calculating dismissiveness. At that moment, I hate him for not taking my grandmother's word. I can hear it in his voice. Yes, you are my mother, but you are a woman. Don't question a man's word if you are a woman.

Do not question a man's word if you are a woman? I become desperate. What am I to do when my word comes up against his? Abuelita Magdalena has always been an honorable woman, yet why does he dishonor her now? Why does he not believe her over Don Rogelio?

Would he ever do to me what Don Rogelio did to his daughter? Is it merely his aura of the day that separates him from the beast he could become?

The day arrives inside my night vision. This is still Mexico City. My consciousness remains trapped in the child, unable to escape back into the woman who sleeps alone in an American city, unable to greet another daylight, to greet a different day in that other dimension. I watch the events of my past unfold and mutate in the multiple currents of time. My mother is tired. She does not want to go out today. My sisters are going to the movies with my cousins, and my brothers are out. They are boys. No one asks where. In the kitchen, I play lotería by myself. My father enters the room.

"Let's go, Magdalena, hija," says my father.

"Where to, papá?"

"We're going to the museum to see the memories of our Indian forefathers."

I go without questioning. A woman's voice enters my dreamscape and says, *"As you are destined to, until you learn the secrets of the Ritual of Restoration, so you can free yourself and us."* The voice. It is familiar. Yet, I can't recognize it. I seem to know something, but what?

The drive is long. I look out the window and watch

the monuments of the fathers: the Indians, the conquistadores, the reformers, the heroes of the endless revolutions. My father looks out the other window. He, too, becomes like those monuments, a mask of heroism and dignity made of strong metal. Time forgives all sins. It is daytime and now my father is with me. I am important to him. That is why he feeds me the memories. He is the keeper of time and reason. This he tells me silently. I can only inherit this world of the fathers through him. Without my connection of him, I am lost forever. I am outcast, a bastard to my name and to the living past of the rotting mercados and solitary palaces that are deprived of their noble lords, of the men who called themselves nobles because they were powerful. Here, on El Paseo de la Reforma, the power of the Spanish forefathers remains forever: destroyers and creators of worlds, of a people.

I become suspended between realities even further because the child that I am in this vision is daydreaming and remembering my uncle Francisco Valencia, a direct descendant of the conquering fathers. Tío Pancho. I hate him.

I think of my cousin Consuelo, his daughter. He says his wife betrayed him with another man and that Consuelo is that man's daughter. So many whispers.

I hear Tía Esperanza's tearful denial — *"Soy mujer honrada...."* Papá and mamá believe Tío Pancho because he is my mother's first cousin and he is a man.

Tío Pancho smells of whiskey all the time. I remember how Tía Esperanza keeps a garden of beautiful mystery. In mind-drift within my dream she takes Consuelo, the baby, amongst the flowers.

"Why do you do it, tía?" I ask.

"So that m'ija will remember me after I am dead," she replies.

"My father takes me to the great city so that I won't forget him," I tell her.

"That's not a woman's remembrance, hija."

Tía knows that I, the woman, the doctor, am listening to her through this child who stands before her within this dream vision. In her blood is the memory of the Indian medicine women, a bruja, my father says. She knows that her life at this moment is my own creation of remembrances. She breaks the stranglehold of the past, violates the events that were, and speaks to me from the other side of death.

"A man's memories only have worth if they are lifeless. Buildings. Monuments. Statues." She cuts a flower and streaks the pollen on my cheek. *"This is a woman's remembrance, the chain of never ending life."*

The baby's green eyes watch Tía with the look of an

old woman.

"One night, I cried under the stars when Consuelo was still inside me," said Tía. *"It was the night Francisco had run off with another woman. He thought the baby wasn't his."*

God! It didn't happen like this! I struggle to break free of this altered memory. I fall into a sea of boiling rocks, into a hot and unrelenting bitterness. I am screaming to someone, a name that will not form. And the echoes answer in Tío Pancho's voice. The echoes are his cries of imagined indignation, of how he has to feed another man's child.

"All lies!" I scream aloud.

"Magdalena, hija, what are you dreaming about?" It is my father's spirit.

Night.

Consuelo's voice: *"Nena, come out here with me."*

"Where are you?"

"Outside. Let's watch the stars."

I linger by the door. In the moonless night she sits among the flowers. An empty haunting of some forgotten dream enters my heart, as if the night were its own language, as if I am being reminded of something important that I should know.

Suddenly I become aware that Consuelo, in her hidden imagination, remembers the secret movements of the stars. But, I have forgotten. A wispy shadow of a memory remains in its place, a starving hunger of nostalgia.

I come out. Sitting next to Consuelo, I watch the lonely lights as they fight the eternal blackness.

"Remember, Nena, when we were kids and how you used to tell me there were people who lived near the second star of the Big Dipper? I was so intrigued that all I wanted to do when I grew up was to build a spacecraft that would take me there." In the dark she becomes a timeless woman that my heart longs to recognize, to know. *"The stars need dreamers to re-invent them. Out there by themselves without companions and without names, waiting for us to love them."* Consuelo laughs. *"You think I am crazy, right?"*

"No, it's not crazy to dream."

Later Consuelo says, *"You should go back to Mexico City to make peace with your memories, Nena."* Her eyes have the same expression as they did that day in her mother's garden, as if she were born with some subversive ability to understand and love. And, later, she asks, *"Nena, do you know how my father feels about me?"*

Reluctantly, I say, *"Yes."*

I don't like thinking about it let alone talk. Tío Pancho cannot forgive the memory of his dead wife. Drunk, he mistakes the daughter for the wife, screams out the rage in his heart. A woman has no right to betray him. He has the blood of the great fathers, he proclaims. His people came to the New World with Balboa, and now this, a treacherous wife . . . .

"I should throw you out into the streets with your bastard," he says, still seeing his wife and not his daughter.

And Consuelo, *"You are sick, papá. Time to sleep."*

For nights, until her untimely death, she helps this drunken mass to his bed, a man still burdened by the memory of his wife, a woman he brutalized because her love had conquered him.

Night after night she takes her father and puts him to bed as if he were a child. She protects him from the solitude of his guilt. This is a ritual. It is the ritual of the fathers, to unequivocally care for them, to protect them from the truth of night.

I, too, understand my responsibilities to the keepers of our past, our fathers.

"You can fight all of your life, not for your father's ac-

ceptance, but for his lack of rejection." Consuelo pauses for a moment and looks back towards the house where Francisco now dreams of Esperanza, the only woman he truly loved.

"Our fathers have been fighting us since the death of the last sun," she says.

Such a dreamer, and a beautiful young woman. A contradiction, to be sure: not a poet but a mathematician, a manipulator of reason, a scientist — like me. I study her face in the shadows and wonder if people consider her eccentric, this strange creator of artificial stars.

"Men are different from women, Nena. They distrust their life-giving forces. They falsely believe that only domination will save them from their mistrust."

In the rivers of time, Consuelo will not see her twenty-eighth birthday. Death condemns her to eternal youth. Yet, for the moment, her smiling green eyes console me.

This night of solitude breaks again with the day and with it vanishes the labyrinth of remembrances. Today, however, in the sanitized sterility of this hospital where I work, the presence of my cousin stays with me during the day. In the daytime the memory of her no longer consoles me. It makes me feel as if there is a secret inside of me. I return to my office. I want to hide for a moment. In the drawer is the album of photographs my mother gave me, the images that I am to remember, official and consecrated. The stiffness of the faces betray nothing except an obsession to conquer. *"Conquer what?"* I ask outloud, with my cousin's voice overlapping mine.

"That girl and her mother are brujas," I hear my father say. Now the insanity of dreams is invading the world of light. Before I can stop it, another vision invades my mind. I see them again in Mexico City, sitting at the table alone, the doctor and his mujer, a unit so synchronized that you forget that they are two beings, rather than a dual monstrosity.

"You see how Esperanza has Francisco bewitched?" my mother says. Her voice melts with contempt. I am confused and afraid. This woman gave me life, yet I smell the warm skin of my aunt and my cousin as once again I become nostalgic. But, for what? Sometimes I think that they — my father and mother — can always see me, even from their resting places of death. I think that they enact this drama of memory for me as I, consumed in this maze of memory and dreams, hide behind the curtain of flower patterns in the house in the great Mexican city. I hide as a child of my dreams. Or I hide as the woman in Houston, the city of glass, hiding in my office while the impatience of the world of reason calls me to the duties of my profession. I listen to their voices and learn the parameters of my obedience.

"Become like Esperanza and later Consuelo and you be-

tray your honor."

"A woman like that makes all of us look like fools," says my mother. She is not anyone's fool. She is her husband's partner. Together they make themselves a royalty. Every year they return to Mexico City as if to proclaim that they are the rightful heirs to the old palace dwellers, as if once they had lived in this former glory and have now been re-born to reclaim it.

"May God help us that none of our children ever shame us," says my mother.

My father hardens. *"All children are traitors to their fathers."*

My mother dares to question him. *"What do you mean, Rodolfo?"*

"I had to betray my father," he explains.

"Yes," counters my mother, *"But he was a...."*

My father says what my mother cannot: *"A lazy, irresponsible drunk. And my mother a saint to maintain our home and our upbringing. But our sons,"* continues my father, *"I can already see their grandfather in them. I tell you right now, they won't get another cent until they've earned my respect. I won't have them drinking and whoring at my expense. I have always maintained the sanctity of my home and wife. Where do these filthy ideas come from?"*

I am now in surgery. Once in a while, my hands become entities upon themselves and perform miracles while women's voices weave a remembrance not mine. Colors and tonal music swirl in my vision. Behind me the memory of my father and mother seem distant. It is as if these women's voices have come to reclaim me, as if I belonged to them. The voices swim in the colors while I remain concealed in the edges of the dream, in a darkness. I am afraid of this shadow, this waking dream. I can break its fragile power with the light.

"Magdalena, hija, turn on the light when you have a bad dream." My father is speaking to me. His voice is young, confident, infallible. Yet, in this waking dream I choose to remain in the dark. I fear, suddenly, the light more than the swirling colors and tonal music of the women. The dream is now ending, dissolving. I try hard to hold on, to decipher one of its secrets. One of the women begins to emerge. I focus her image as my father's stern voice rises to warn me, *"Beware of women's witchery!"*

I fear the face coming into focus, as though it will incarnate the deformities of my father's given fears. The vision is ending. Consuelo emerges. Consuelo, the young and beautiful dreamer. *"Nena, the hidden city awaits."*

Chapter Two

Mexico City

Time has piled upon time. Just as papá said. He spoke the truth. Down the Paseo de la Reforma the bronze statues watch me with dead eyes. Here, the past never dies. The lives of the dead are frozen in another dimension and watch the Now through sad and greedy eyes. Only the Now is alterable. The rest of time is still within its own defeated fate. I am remembering everything my papá has said as he and I walked down this street.

"Hija, this is your heritage. Of all of my children, you understand the best. I have chosen you to carry me after I am dead."

"Why, papá? I am a girl and the youngest. That honor belongs to my brother."

"No, hija. Sometimes one has to change things so that

they can continue. Every tradition was once new and radical."

The unsmiling statues continue to watch.

"What of the statues, papá? What of the dead fathers?"

"They will die without you, hija."

They may die with me. The years have passed, and I, the bearer of my family name, by choice I have remained alone and childless. Perhaps I want to end this curse of remembrance. Dios mío, if I could only forget.

I take a cab to the neighborhood where my father was born. My abuelita Magdalena's house has been sold. On the lower floor is a cheap shoe store. Upstairs I hear the screams of crying children. They are the new tenants. I walk away in an effort to erase this new hallucination of reality and to restore my memories of the house, the smell of my grandmother. A cab driver pulls up. I shake my head and walk back to La Zona Rosa where I have been staying. The people at the hotel have been worried.

"Doctor, we thought the worst had happened!"

They have known my family since the death of my grandmother. That was the first time my family stayed in this hotel. The same people still work there. I return to this hotel year after year, as if I am bound to these people. They have been my phantom family, watching me grow into this respectable death.

I dream dreams that I can't remember when I awake. Only the smell of flowers remains streaked across my face. I go to breakfast. I have determined to rid myself of this irritation, these dreams that become incarnate as my young cousin. Determined, I tell myself, "You must forget your guilt. You cannot change the fact that Consuelo defied her father with that incident with Jeff." What a shame! What caused her to commit such an indiscretion so openly, I don't know. You cannot have a blemish against you, never. Now, Tío Pancho screams in a euphoria of alcohol, *"A man can roll in the dirt, but not a woman!"* And I couldn't bring myself to defend her. Consuelo is lost for an unmarked eternity, and it is horrible to love an absence. Time means nothing.

"It is not your fault that your father disgraced himself," I explain to myself. He deceived and exploited his own people. That was his own choice, not yours. You had to think of your own reputation. How could you defend him when your own memories demanded justice? How could you defend him when you had to feel their shame because they had forgotten how the indignities of poverty felt. How they despised the poor who came to them only because their tongues were imprisoned in Spanish. Mistakenly, the people believed that a doctor who spoke their own tongue would be more compassionate than an Americano.

The fire was an accident. These tragedies touch us all. All of us, Doctor Magdalena. Be reasonable! Reasonable? Reason is my salvation. Reason has its limits, and it limits the sea of uncertainty. Reason is the line on the beach that proclaims to the ocean, only to this point may you wreak your chaos of devastation. Without reason I am, I am, I ... am ....

"Doctor Magdalena?"

It is that waiter that my father liked so much. Don Enrique. He is a pristine embodiment of our customs: clean and respectable, a creature of the proprieties of the day. I wonder what don Enrique would sound like and look like in one of the brothels. I had wondered that about my father, but he was not like other men. For him, there were never any brothels or other women or even flirtations. There was only his mujer, his wife. My father was a wonder among men of power. He was the perfected ideal of men: power and the self-execution of the most rigorous morals. Among his peers, the latter made him untouchable, even god-like. Never would they find Doctor Rodolfo Ibarra drunk in a bordello, a fool born to prove that we are all fools, and weak behind our masks. Don Enrique, the waiter, is that superficial exterior of don Rodolfo. He is an illusion of my father.

The endless chatter of this waiter pollutes my resolve of reason above all. I want to be alone to distill the waking dreams from my consciousness.

"We are very sorry about your parents, pues es que lo sentimos mucho...."

My silence manages to exile this irritating apparition called don Enrique. But the delicate network of my reason has been disrupted, my mind wanders, time remains still, my organism remains suspended in that other unreality that desires food and sleep and love. I look at the artificial flowers on the table. They were created by the hands of the poor Indians who wander into the city that they recognize in their visions. Beneath the concrete nightmare are the canals filled with perfumed flowers, the swept streets of volcanic stone, the faces of the watchful gods. That is the city they see. I watch the Indians from my table at the hotel restaurant. Their impoverished clothing conceals their magnificence, as if they wish to remain invisible from the rest of us. But I can see them now, not as caricatures of the nightmare of steel and concrete. Rather, I see them as they really are. They have defied time and co-exist with us in their own reality. Their multi-colored clothes are a code more profound than spoken language. In it — the dancing pattern of swirling colors — oh God, I never realized . . . .

"Me compra estas flores, señorita?"

The Indian woman is old, but she is not like the usual street vendor. Standing before me, she patiently waits for me, as if she is waiting for me to acknowledge her secret identity.

"Compreme estas flores. Soy muy pobre."

I have escaped from my imagination, from the dimension that I was.... No! That is unreasonable! This woman wears the same multi-colored clothing of invisibility. She holds the flowers before me. Time has stopped. The flowers are eternal because they have been created by the hand of the old woman. Yet, their illusory existence yearns for nostalgia, for the possibilities of my memories. If only Consuelo were here . . . . Why does this old woman remind me of her?

At this moment, as I am watching the old woman, she weaves me into another dimension. I am awake. I watch her remain suspended in one reality, offering me her flowers, while I and my young cousin in another, roam an ancient mercado by a lake.

"Nena, look!" Consuelo runs up to me. She is now an adolescent, a magnificent creature between innocence and corruption. *"Nena, let's buy these flowers."*

I answer her in a forgotten language I cannot comprehend.

Consuelo smiles at me. *"The flowers of forgetfulness, Nena."*

"¿Qué hace aquí?" The waiter Enrique demands as he grabs the old flower woman. The spell of the living night is broken. I remain shocked by this intrusion into the old woman's spell. Brusquely, Enrique shoves the woman out. He shows no sympathy, not even for the humiliation because of her years.

"I'm so sorry, Doctor Ibarra. These beggars have no respect for anything."

"Why did you treat that old woman like that?" I say unthinking, still wounded by the vision of the old woman.

Enrique, embarrassed, says something to me, and in my confusion of languages, of realities, I cannot understand his words, his concerns, and I walk out of the hotel restaurant to pursue the old woman who seduced me with her benevolent hallucination.

"Time has piled upon time. Down the Paseo de la Reforma the bronze statues watch me with dead eyes. Here, the past never dies. The lives of the dead are frozen in another dimension and watch the Now through sad and greedy eyes."

Chapter Three

El Mercado

Though old, the flower woman easily outpaces me. I run after her through the multitudes. Still, she slowly disappears. Meanwhile, the sun heats the gray air with malicious indifference. I want to stop and go inside somewhere and get a cold drink. I want to sit in an air-conditioned room and say, "Doctor Magdalena, you tried to help an old woman's poverty. You are compassionate, but not unreasonable. There are beggars by the thousands in this city, an absurd impossibility of misery. As a doctor, you want to help. That old woman is like the others you will meet. Give generously to the next one. In the end, it will all be the same."

The old woman climbs into a bus. I hail a taxi.

"Where is that bus going, joven?"

The young man's green eyes are not perplexed, as if

he expected the absurdity of my question. "Al Mercado de la Merced," he replies as he opens the door of the car. I, as if privy to some unwritten conspiracy, climb in and watch the city of statues vanish behind me. If I do not acknowledge them, if I do not worship their memory, their solidity melts. For the moment, the torture of my responsibility to the memory of the fathers is defeated. I am moving towards the center of the universe, towards a city by a forgotten lake.

I am lost in the mercado, for it has no end. The paths behind me now vanish and I cannot get back. My reason tells me: This cannot be, turn back, go back, Doctor Ibarra, you need help, you are tortured by the death of your parents whom you abandoned. They died in their home, consumed by fire, the neighbors watched in horror, the fire was too intense, the firefighters were beaten back by the fury, the screams penetrated the night, **"¡Magdalena, Hija! M-a-g-d-a-le-n-a-a-a-a"**

And now I pursue some phantom, a woman my father would call a whore of the mind, a superstitious vieja. I want to turn back, I want to. Then Consuelo's voice instructs, *"This way, Nena."* The mercado becomes less recognizable, all of the traces of modernity have disappeared.

I walk past a vendor of candles, he calls out to me, *"Compreme estas velas, señorita. They are the blessed souls of your children."*

Another vendor, a young Indian boy, like the others, calls out to me in a melodic Spanish with an Indian accent. *"Se vende sueño y sueños. Adelante, señorita. Sleep and dreams for sale."*

I am passing another old woman, extremely old, as if she had defeated death, as if at the last moment she became eternal. She sits on the ground, silent, but, as I pass her, she, too, calls out in a voice that matches her ancient countenance. *"Se vende olvido."*

"¿Qué dice?" I ask. A vertigo of heat begins to form inside my head.

"Se vende olvido. Pase, señorita. Pase."

Olvido. Forgetfulness.

And then the voice of my young cousin, this time mature as the young woman she was at the time of her death. *"These flowers are beautiful, Nena. They have more life in them, although they are dead.... "*

The old woman has been speaking to me through this dream of vertigo, showing me some dried flowers in a jar. *"These dried flowers, mija, have the power to remove your memory. That is what you came looking for, isn't it? Didn't you say, 'Dios mío, if only I could forget?'"*

"No!" I protest. *"I am looking for an old Indian woman. I followed her from La Zona Rosa — "*

I stop in mid-sentence. My reason awakens and reveals my own absurdity. This is a mercado full of Indians. The identity of the old woman has melted into this mass of humanity, a humanity lost and unseen by my world of machines and concrete.

"What is this place?" I am dissolving into a painless dimension, into the vortex.

"This is the mercado of miracles, hija," explains the old woman.

"I don't understand, señora. Are you a curandera?"

"Some in your world call me that. To others, I am a bruja. My people call me La Doña of Forgetfulness because my husband was the Trickster of Forgetfulness."

A curtain of blackness falls upon me. No longer do I hear the old woman as I lapse into a visionless night.

"Isn't it wonderful,Nena?" says Consuelo's voice. I enter my dream of the endless void. My final thought is a quote from Doctor Samuel Johnson: *"Wonder is a pause of reason."*

Chapter Four

The Land of the Ancients

I have dreamt of nothing for the first time since the death of my parents. How long ago —how long have I slept? How long have they been dead? I don't remember. My name? Think: Magdalena. Magdalena, temptress of the saints my abuelito Rodolfo used to say. Grandfather. My father. This blackness does not move, nor does it breathe. There is no light and the absence of sound, silence, sound's darkness. Where am I?

An old woman's voice says, *"You are in the house of the ancients. Awake now, hija."*

My eyes open. I see the interior of a house repeated a million times — the whitewashed adobe walls, that smell of the earth, the high ceilings where myriad birds find refuge in the winter, the iconography of Christian saints on the walls, furniture from a generic past. Every old adobe house since the arrival of the Spanish fathers retains this saddened look, as if it is the face of an old woman multiplied to watch the souls of us, her children. I could be anywhere: in Coahuila in the north or in El Valle de Santiago outside of Mexico City, Guanajuato, Veracruz. The air of heated dust and smoking oil lamps are the same, obliterating geography and time. I am within five hundred years.

I turn and look upon the face who possesses that voice that speaks to me. Some foreign knowledge inside my head tells me, *"This is La Doña del Olvido, the lady of forgetfulness."* I don't know how I know this. She has the look of an ageless saint, as if she were forgotten by God and left on earth with all of her desires for union with the Eternity intact.

Another old woman enters the room. She is the flower woman from La Zona Rosa. I am confused by the memory.

"You fainted in the mercado," says the one called La Doña. *"Mi comadre Manuela and I brought you home ...."*

I interrupt. *"Where is this place? Are we in a colonia outside the city?"*

Manuela the flower woman winces. *"She retains her power of reason. It will be a problem."*

"It is a risk, comadre, but Consuelo insisted that her reason be left intact."

"What? My cousin Consuelo! Are you mad? She died — six months ago, I think." Inside my head the pain increases and my stomach wants to empty itself. La Doña brings me a cup of tea.

"Hija ...."

"Where am I, señora?"

The two women exchange a brief glance. La Doña replies, *"You are in the stream of time from which you came, you are now in the American city. You left the mercado on the same day that you arrived. Manuela ...."*

Manuela goes to an ancient dresser and takes out a small, gold framed mirror, like the one Hernan Cortés used to deceive the Indians. I look into the mirror and the city of Houston appears, and I am there, going through the routines of my life with a fatalistic indifference. Suddenly, I am conscious that I am actually **there**!

"Where am I?" I repeat, suddenly fearful that I am insanely trapped inside one of my hallucinating visions.

"Here and there, hija. Once the woman in the mirror came to us in the mercado of miracles and asked us to remove her memory because she could no longer bear the weight of her dreams and guilt. She was merely seeking forgetfulness and

did not remember the prophecy given to her at another time, long before this time.

The one who is now called Magdalena Ibarra was destined to return to us, but we could not keep her for more than a short moment of time. So we removed her memory and returned her to the world that is seen so that no one would suspect our presence. It is very important that the seen world does not discover my people. Not yet."

"What is this? A dream?" I ask.

"No, hija. It is real. It is another reality that your mirror woman fears to see, but you still control who you are in this — what can I call it so you will understand — this aberration in the planes of time and being."

"If the woman in the mirror is me, then what am I, here, now?"

"You are Magdalena Ibarra's tonalli. The other ...."

"Ay, I wish that it were so," I reply. *"Perhaps I am dreaming again, and desire to be free of the emptiness in my life. Maybe I am dead, and even here, in death, I am still deprived of rest."*

La Doña takes my hand and caresses it. *"Hija, your reason makes it hard for you to understand, but where you are right now, here, this place, is a world that only few can see between their dreams. Once, long ago, you were a kinswoman of our people. We, my comadre and Consuelo and you, were given a gift by the first gods who lived in the caves and the trees. It is they who taught us the secrets of time. You are called a Dreamer, and only the greatest of dreamers can cross the worlds of time. We sent you through time, you and Consuelo, to restore us — the keepers of the old medicine — to visibility when the time of our death arrived. But Consuelo was taken too soon, her baby, too, who was destined to be a great man."*

I watch the dark eyes of the old woman and dissolve into her rivers. Suddenly, my heart opens up, my defiant reason is defeated for a moment.

"If what you say is true, I don't understand it."

La Doña continues. *"Hija, you cannot possibly remember because centuries ago we removed your memory before we sent you out. You asked that of us, back then. Perhaps it is your weakness for forgetfulness, perhaps there is a special medicine for your recovery of memory. We do not know. You, Consuelo, and my husband the Trickster, were the most secretive of our people and the most powerful. The Trickster was a god and was punished by the other gods for consorting with me. Neither he nor you and Consuelo were allowed to share your secrets with the rest of us.*

I can only tell you what I know, the rest you must discover by yourself. You and Consuelo were the only keepers of the Ritual of Restoration, but Consuelo died with a child within her ....

During the Fourth Sun, our people were called the Keepers. We were a great and powerful tribe, but mysterious even to the new gods because the first ones, the very old gods, the gods of caves and trees, had given us the secrets of the great creation.

When the Fifth Sun arrived, the gods dissolved our unity as a tribe. The new gods feared the ancient gods, however, and they did not kill us. Instead, they made us the vendors of magic in the mercados of Tenochtitlan. We became the greatest of all curanderos. Even the Aztec priests were envious of our power. Then, when the men on horseback arrived, the old gods sent us into the secret cave of time, to this place which takes up the same space as the seen world. But this one is invisible. It was the only way to survive, for the god of the horsemen was madly jealous and would have destroyed our people and, therefore, our knowledge.

It was then that we were given a prophecy: our existence in the cave of time would be a Sun or five centuries from the arrival of the white man. After the passage of this era of the Sun, we were to be restored to the seen world by a Dreamer. The Dreamers are the only ones of our people who know the ritual. If we are not restored, we will die. And our secrets of healing will die with us. The seen world is sick and needs us, but we cannot become visible without the Ritual of Restoration.

Before the gods made us invisible, the horsemen killed all but two of our Dreamers, you and Consuelo. I, the chief tribes-

woman and the wife of the Trickster, sent you both through time, to be born of the blood of the horsemen so you'd be unharmed and could return safely when the time of restoration arrived.

Consuelo's mother was the traveler. She knew about both worlds and prepared you — your conscience, for you must be of a pure heart. Consuelo understood that she had to come to us with child, for his afterbirth was needed. How? I do not know exactly. Only she and you know the secret. But she was killed.

Your visions and dreams, we have been sending them to you but your father had trained you to be ashamed of what he called woman's witchery and superstition. You resisted us, denied us in your dreams and in your guilt over your father's sins. When your father died, we asked his spirit to call you, and he did, for his blood is that of the Teotihuacanos."

"Why," I ask, "would my father's spirit agree when he always despised what he called superstition?"

"He has his own reason," says La Doña. *"His ambitions rage even in death."*

I go to the window, throw it open and see the untouched land, a wilderness beyond time. Or so it seems, for I do not recognize it. On the other side of the house, however, I can hear the cries of the mercado, and I can smell a humanity mingled with dust and sun.

"I was in Mexico City," I say in a flash of memory. *"I was in a mercado."*

"Yes," says La Doña. *"Manuela, the messenger, took you there."*

"Then I heard Consuelo" I recall, *"—saw her—Consuelo died last year. It was an accident, I think. Yes, that was it. An accident."*

"We, my comadre Manuela and I, we are sorry that we had to send the spirit of your cousin to get you. When we first sent the spirit of your father, you resisted him. That is why we then asked La Muerte to give us the spirit of Consuelo during the night."

"Will I see her again?"

"You want that very much, don't you?"

"Yes. She was more like a sister to me. Then I became ashamed of what people said of her, and I stayed away. I never saw her again."

"She knows how your pride defeated your heart. But she loves you even in death, Doctor. You will see her, but only at night, and only when she calls you."

I look in the mirror again and watch the night descend upon the city of Houston and my other self sleeps like an innocent. I look around and the old women have disappeared. I am shifted as if in a dream, in an absurd reality that violates the order of the empirical world. Life in this place functions as a dream, where the logic of linear time is non-existent. Days have passed in a single moment, and I do not know what has become of them. It is now night, and I am alone.

Then her voice! It is as icy as the night, *"Magdalena! Ay, Nena! Mi hijo! My son —* ***Save him! Nena!"***

A flood of memory invades me, the memories that have been removed from my other. I am seized by those things that my heart has always desired: my grandfather's face, the warmth of the sun coming through a churchyard, the smell of unmoved air in the old sector of Mexico City, the lands of my imagination as a child, the voice of Consuelo as we talk outside of her father's house in Los Angeles, the hum of the city's malevolence that cannot touch us — women like Consuelo and me.

I am trying to make sense of this spinning world, where all things exist at once, all time, all desires, all memory. Yes, now I can remember. I came into a mercado, became lost because Consuelo led me into its depths, and I was suddenly surrounded by merchants who offered me what I most desired: Sueño y sueños — sleep and dreams, the souls of my future children, the kiss of my beloved within the secret of night, and what I most wanted — olvido, forgetfulness.

All I wanted was forgetfulness. I wanted to forget

the chains that my father commanded me to wear in his honor, to do him honor. I wanted to forget my mother's arrogance as she sent the poor away from my father's office because they could not pay. I wanted to forget those faces, pleading, defeated, reduced to an existence of dying animals because my father and mother denied them the cure of his hands. My father, the good doctor. The good father who never dishonors his wife and family, who honors them with selfish greed and self-proclaimed righteousness. He is never wrong, no, and his shadow, my mother, with her constancy, pulls him deeper into his righteous malice.

I wanted to forget the hardness of their faces as they sent away the old women and the injured men, the children fatigued by ailments which my father's eyes could discern and cure with the magic of his hands. I wanted to forget my shameful legacy.

Consuelo's clear voice pierces through the spell of memories, *"Nena, is it true that you are going to med school just to right your father's wrongs?"*

And I: *"It tortures me like a disease inside my head. I feel as if they — the people my parents rejected — are wandering through the shadows of reality, waiting there to seize me, to kill me and thus atone for them. I have to find them in other faces, Consuelo. ."*

"You can never atone for them. You can never undo what

they did. It is final. Their sins, not yours, Nena."

I am swirled into another past. I am too young to be in school, so my mother, who works as my father's office manager, takes me to work with her. I sit in my father's office, coloring a book. An old man, with the gaunt smile of one used to humiliations, comes in with his wife. The woman's kind eyes look at me and even then my healer's imagination tells me what her illness is.

The old man's voice is directed to my mother. *"My wife. She has hurt her hip. She is in a lot of pain, señora. Can Doctor Ibarra see her?"*

"You'll need to deposit fifteen dollars for the consultation," my mother informs him.

The old man and his wife exchange a look of desperation. He turns to my mother, *"I can ask the man where I wash dishes if he can advance me five dollars."*

"The doctor will see you if you pay the fifteen dollars first."

The old man and his wife walk out. The waiting room is still with the hot breathing of the other patients, knowing that they have cheated the humiliation of poverty for one moment. They, too, are like the old man and his wife, except that they understand life better than to ask for kindness. I look at the faces and a woman bursts out laughing. *"Stupid kid,"* she ridicules me, *"your father is a bastard and your mother a devil of greed !"*

I had to go to medical school. There was no other way to undo their sins. But, at the same time, I had to let them think that I was doing it for their honor, not their sins. *"You are the best of our children,"* said Doctor Rodolfo Ibarra. *"You shall be the best of us, your father and mother. You shall have and be everything we cannot create for ourselves. You shall be our greatest creation."*

But I wanted to be the creation that I desired for them: a doctor who wants to heal the human flesh because it contains pieces of all of our collective dreams, because all flesh is a piece of me.

Consuelo's voice floats back. *"That's wonderful, Nena. It's good to know I'm not the only crazy woman in this family of ours."*

Night in the adobe house. Outside, disembodied cries are carried by the wind, a chorus of voices, men and women. *"Ay, you have power over death, Doctor Magdalena!"*

I am the memories of Magdalena Ibarra, the Dreamer removed from the world of stainless steel and machines. All of my memories, even the dreams I am to dream tonight are held inside my head, ready to emerge. What chaos is this? What is the name of my home? I live.... I live....where? A city of glass....

Time has passed. I don't know how it is that at the last moment I was newly arrived in the cave of time and now weeks have gone by. Many nights I hear the wails of my cousin who is sentenced to muteness when she sees me, so I cannot talk with her, so she cannot help me remember the ritual. But I can hear the wails. I can only be with her, watch the stars with her and understand why she wails at night, for the spirit of her child drifts, homeless, through the heavens. Consuelo and I go into the desert to watch the stars, or we go into an ancient Arabic-like Hispanic city beside the mercado, and there, when I look in many mirrors, I see myself in the city of glass, a woman without a memory.

The city of glass: Houston. There, a phantom of my dream-self continues to live and work — exist. The woman of the city calls up the gifts of her education — a brilliant thinker, yes, I admire myself within my image self, brilliant thinker, so self-contained, respected by the world of machinery and digital logic. Everything is 0-1. I am now perfect in the world of 0-1. No longer haunted by the guilt and memory of my past. My digital woman has won her peace of mind because she has left a piece of her mind — her tonalli —me — the image of self, here, where I float in a river of memory and forgetfulness. One moment I recreate lives not mine, a past remembered in my blood, the old people, my ancestors, and the next moment I am seized by the disease of forgetfulness, and Manuela, with La Doña, consume my memory. They dream my dreams for me so that I can journey into a dream of spinning blackness and meet — I am journeying — somewhere, but the pain of the nightmare defeats me again.

La Doña is sitting next to me, stroking my head. *"Hija, you nearly lost your soul."*

"I felt the hand of death," I say. I am not at all surprised by my unscientific observation.

"You must try to enter the vortex again soon, or you and all of us will be lost, erased from the rivers of time. I must tell you, our time is almost up."

There is not much time left, and the spell of forgetfulness has afflicted even my tonalli self. If my reason had been totally removed, then perhaps I could remember the ritual. But Consuelo's spirit said no —. There are many things I do not understand here in this restful desert between two times, between the rivers of death and life. Sometimes, at night, I sense a coldness. It is foreign to the living, as if hell were a glacier that vomits it souls into the moonless nights. The secrets and the answers to my unformed questions lie in my deepest dreams which are like pleasant journeys, forgotten as soon as they are remembered. How sweet is forgetfulness, even for me.

As I am dreaming, I feel the women's ritual, the consuming of my dreams, as if they were a dream themselves. Sometimes I am afraid of sleeping, not because of them, but because I am afraid to wake up reunited with my other self in Houston. Once again the woman is tormented by memories, by the mask of tradition, respect, and duty. My other self is happy without me; she is now the perfect daughter of Doctor Rodolfo Ibarra. She is a skilled technician, a scientist who has mastered precision, a woman of reasonable conscience. That is good.

I awake. I had been dreaming again. The kinswomen are gone. I go out into the mercado. There, a blind boy offers to sing to me.

"If I only had some money...." I begin to say, and suddenly memory seizes me and I recall that money comes once a week. Money that my other self sends to these women without knowing why. I give the boy five dollars, American money.

He sings me a song about me, about the meaning of my dreams, the meaning of the spell of forgetfulness. As he is singing, his words turn into swirls of color that I cannot interpret. Dusk descends like a song that has been sung in the distance, then carried by the birds and the wind. I decide not to return to my kinswomen for now. I've no desire to sleep in their protection as they enchant my dreams from me, then materialize them as ghosts. I know that they desire to know my secrets of healing, that perhaps the chaos of my mind will betray the magic they need for their restoration — I still cannot recover my forgotten secret. I cannot. The mercado remains timeless, as if it were the same mercado in all of time and transposed through space. How wonderful. I go into the mercado and wander to its end.

The old Arabic-Hispanic city sits peacefully at the edge of the mercado. It reminds me of the city of Guanajuato at night , with people who crowd its streets, liberated from their worldly responsibilities by the coming of darkness. Caught in the night are the collective odors of all the foods eaten, of all the possibilities of love, and of all the songs sung simultaneously. They reach into the darkened canopy and join in a desperate chaos.

I wander, lost in the pathos of memory and in the serenity of the night that ultimately has descended upon the city. I am free to admit my own secrets, my failings. Here they do not torment me. I wonder if this is hell. Perhaps the torments of hell are merely of our own creation, for here I refuse the law of my fathers and there is no retribution. I do not regret the smell of my beloved on my skin, nor the betrayal of my father — the lawsuit. How could I defend him?

My mother admonishes, *"If you don't testify on your father's behalf, we shall be ruined."*

"You have ruined yourselves ...."

"You would do this to us, who loved you better than our other children, who gave you our best? It is because of our children, especially you, that we did what we did."

"I won't be responsible for your decisions. Papá could have — you could have — been more generous, perhaps even tried to exhibit some compassion."

"Do you think you could have had what you had — your good life and education — if we had given away your father's valuable time? There will always be the poor. Your father and I determined that our children would not live the lives of dogs."

"Why must you be so disrespectful of poor people, mamá? You and papá treated them like the dogs you speak about, when you know that they trusted papá. He was one of their people. He spoke their tongue. They merely wanted what you wanted, a better life. What's wrong with that?"

"The only thing wrong, Magdalena, is your refusal to stand up for your father."

And I did not, for he and my mother had taught me only too well. My respect among my peers was more important than anything else. By not testifying for my father, I chose myself over them. But that is merely a technicality, for, in truth, my father deserved justice. His conviction was suspended, but he lost his license to practice medicine. Worse, he lost his honor. But then, a woman and her child died because of my father's lack of care. Who cares? Who cares? They breed like animals, make our people look bad. They drop their children in the fields like the Indians that they are. A woman and her child. A year later my beloved cousin, six months pregnant, was accidentally shot by her half-brother, a bullet intended for their father, Francisco Valencia. The bastard son was trying to kill his father. He shot the woman savior instead, killed her son of redemptions, still warm and wet within her womb. The ambulance arrived late, too late. Perhaps someone had thought, *"Pay no attention, it's those poor dogs again. Let them kill themselves, poor bastards, we're better off without one more."* Perhaps not. Perhaps another woman and her child needed to leave the earth, create a second void, one that I cannot fill in spite of all of my attempts at propitiation.

"Señorita?"

An old man, his eye destroyed by the disease of neglect, his face eroded by time, offers me some roses.

"¿Cuanto, señor?"

He hands them to me, a gift. I take them because I have learned not to reject the gifts of the invisible people. They remind me of the very people I had ceased to help because somewhere in my life I let the fires of idealism be quenched by pragmatism. *"How, hija real de tu padre, is that different from your father's way?"*

I stop at a refreshment stand. As I drink, I notice the man next to me. He is selling the candy of the dead, the sweetness of sugar sculpted into the many images of death.

"Señorita, buy one of these candies and tonight you will revisit your dead."

I look at his offerings. A solitary man with a skull face. A coffin with a woman and a baby inside. A man with a demon face followed by a woman devil. Two skeletons dancing while a skeleton mariachi plays. A flash of boiling blood invades my brain.

"No, gracias," I say as I turn away. The man calls out to me. *"You'll dream about it anyway, so take the magic."*

Quickly, I run from him.

"¡Señorita! Eat the candies!"

I run to the entrance of a tunnel that descends under a road. I see the dim lights of another mercado, even more removed from where I was, a mini-city, a chaos of images, a cold smell. The smell is like an operating room after the death of a patient. I look around as if to find Consuelo. A girl is standing before me, holding up a piece of lace. She moves her lips as if to offer me the lace, but there is only silence, no words emerge. The chaotic choir of the underground mercado increases. Mesmerized, I stare into the pattern of the lace.

I see his face again. I see it as it was ten years ago. Esteban! I feel his words so close to me, that same wonder so long forgotten. He takes my hands and puts them on his face. *"Create me, Magdalena,"* he says, repeating the same wish as if I were a medieval magician who could impress a good fate upon his face and thereby keep him safe from untimely death or sorrow. I see the pattern of these memories of me, but they are not mine. They are Esteban's memories as he dreams of me still, after ten years. I take the lace, pay the girl twice its worth and return to my kinswomen.

Even a land of dreams has its sun and moon and the stars cover the sky like a storm. La Doña and la comadre Manuela are waiting for me. I feel the comfort of the desert at night. As I turn, I see Consuelo. Again, she has been waiting for me. Consuelo takes my hand. She seems desperate to tell me something, looks into my eyes and sees the remnants of my vision of Esteban.

I dream that my kinswomen have created a portal with my lace. In my dream, Esteban is waiting for me on the other side. *"Enter,"* Consuelo says. If the light of the stars could be sound, it would be her voice. I walk through the pattern of lace and Esteban is there, now, as he should look for his age. He holds some clay.

"Nena, make me something. Anything. An animal, a per-

son, a thing. Create something for me."

"I can't," I say. *"I am not an artist."*

"Your hands have always had magic. I hear you can bring the dead back to life, Doctor Magdalena. Just make something for me, if you still love me."

He begins to fade before my eyes. *"Please stay, Esteban. Let me see you, at least. Tell me if you're well, if you are happy. Tell me if you have found someone else. I won't be hurt if you've found someone. I haven't, Esteban. Please don't go just yet."*

His apparition hands me the clay, but before he dissolves he becomes Rey Mendoza, Consuelo's half-brother, Francisco's bastard son. I awake.

La Doña and Manuela are gone. The door has been left open and the sounds of the night's celebration enter the house. The smell of flowers, with their uncontrollable scramble of odors, penetrates me. The smell of perfumes has always made me dizzy. Moving outside, I travel towards the fringes of the Arabic-Hispanic city. A procession goes by. People are masked, music hangs on the edges of the horizon. The Day of the Dead. I had forgotten. My dead — I must — I walk into the chaos. The spinning sickness begins to grip my head and stomach. If only I could find La Doña. She could give me something, some herb of painless sleep that frees this alarm from my flesh, this panic of pain, this sickness of mine, vertigo. I go deeper into the city. There, as before, stands the man with the roses. He sees me, nods, smiles as if he were a traveler of the dimension of fate, and he knew mine. I see another procession. At the end of the train of celebrants are three women, masked as the others, but I recognize them by their ages, two very old women and the third is young. They begin to descend into the tunnel, the underground mercado where I bought the lace.

It is then that I see the young woman lift her mask. It is Consuelo, and her eyes are filled with mourning. I run after her, try to catch up before she disappears into the tunnel, but I can't. She and the others are gone. I look everywhere, but I cannot see them. The coldness of dead blood grips the entrance of the tunnel. And there is another odor, warm and sweet, mixed with smoke and ashes. A force inside my heart, still sick from the apparition of a man I once loved, makes me follow the sweet smoke. I find myself in front of a candy stand, candies made of cacti, and desert flowers, sugar canes and pecans, and yes, the candies of the dead. A man emerges from the back of a stall. It is the same candy vendor I had met earlier.

"Ah, señorita, so you've changed your mind. As beautiful as these are, they are not the right candies."

He parts a curtain and disappears into the back, then reappears with the candies he had offered me before: it was the woman with the dead child in the coffin; a solitary man with a skull's face; the man with the devil face followed by a female demon; and a skeleton mariachi.

"It is the Day of the Dead, señorita. Our dead parents deserve our respects first." He hands me the sculpture of the devil-faced man and his female companion. *"Here, these belong on the grave of your parents."*

I look at the figurines and realize that the secrets of my heart have been exposed. For in my heart, this is how I saw my parents' sins, dark and grotesque. Yes, the vendor is right. I take the candy and a secret voice escapes me and I ask, *"Where is the cemetery, señor?"*

"Through that exit," he replies as he points to a stairway that ascends into another street.

I climb the stairs and come to a street. This part of the city is less exotic, seeming more like the small cities of northern Spain. There is a plaza and a kiosk, empty, but as if it awaits someone, perhaps a band, to play sad songs. Or perhaps it awaits a poet who will read dirges to the dead. Possibly it merely waits for the spirits of those dead whose unfulfilled love haunts their disembodied memories, the spirits who had thought that love was possible only in the flesh, only to react with astonishment upon discovering that the pleasure of the flesh is subordinate, a follower and not the leader of love.

The sad trees bend to cover the heads of the mourners who are exhausted with happiness, for they have revisited their loved ones. I pass the plaza and walk down a cobbled stone street worn by centuries of daily use, outliving the arrogant imagination of the city's builders.

The conquerors never imagined their cities and language and customs as something consumed by the Indians, an impregnation that came to fruition centuries later. They are there, the conquerors, in the hardness of the rock, iron, and stones, in the proud facades of another world, Spain, a world that stares defiantly through the windows of time.

Yes, they, too, have survived, have allowed this impregnation of an Indian dream, wanting it, for they, the Spaniards, also had dreamt of a city of gold across the vastness of the ocean. And the Indians were a people who longed for its conquering son, a Sun, another world.

But the world never dies into oblivion. The world is born again as itself and as another; the two dreams, the opposite dreams, collide in the dimensions of space to fulfill the union of reality, sleep, desire, and pulsing obsession.

Here, on this street, I see the resolution of the two dreams: the eternal Arabic-Hispanic city that celebrates a festival of the Indians. Tonight, in this resolution, I confront the one who gave me this inheritance, the fusion of two worlds. Tonight, I shall see my father.

I walk towards the outer edge of this mythic city, to where the desert encroaches upon this dream. On the hill before me is a cemetery, desolate and sad. It is the burial grounds of my people, the Ibarras and the Valencias. No one has been there to pay their respects to the dead, for my dead did not respect life when they were living. The few dreamers among these two families were ridiculed, beaten, relegated to a life of silent and uncommunicative isolation. Still, the desire for another dreamer remained, and perhaps the next generation would bring a strong savior who would rescue all. Consuelo's son would have been that man for the Valencias, and perhaps Esteban's and my son would have redeemed the Ibarras. But there are no such sons. There are only their would-be mothers, now lost between the mountains of imagination and time.

A rusted wrought iron fence surrounds the cemetery and I am alone with my dead. The desert has decayed and absorbed the dead. Their tombstones have been erased of names and dates. The crosses have been rotted by the sun. Many of the original mounds have collapsed, as if the dead have been sucked back into the earth. Towards the far edge of my private cemetery are two new graves. My recent dead are there, and the graves are open, waiting for me to look. I will not, for I know what I will see: in one I will see the charred remains of my lifegivers; in the other, a young woman clutching her dead child, protecting him forever. I take the candy figurines and place them on the ground. They — and I am no longer surprised by anything — walk into the grave. At that moment, the grave vomits out fire. I look towards the city now wrapped in its cloak of twilight. The lights are coming on, making it a jewel of white dots against the blue of the darkening sky. Slowly the city becomes distorted. The earth opens her mouth and begins to swallow it. She swallows the desert and the sky. The stars, too, become threatened and are subsequently swallowed. Then, constellations beyond our technology's sight and beyond the farthest stretches of our imagination appear before my eyes. In an instant they, too, are consumed by this earth. Only the blackest space remains, absolute nothingness.

At my parents' grave, the fire turns into a liquid of ever-changing colors. I can see the silhouettes of my parents behind this curtain of colors. The sound of horses caught in a rainstorm echoes against the colors.

"I've come to honor your memory, papá, mamá."

Only my father speaks. *"Magdalena, hija, we've waited for you. Free us so we may rest."*

"Free you from what? Your sins? I can't pay for those."

"All children have the power to redeem the sins of their fathers. Even in death there are prisons with doors. You have the power of life and death."

"I have been told that by the mercado people. I have heard the legend sung by the blind boy, but I have no special knowledge, papá. I cannot free you any more than I can restore the people of the old women."

"No!" says my father. *"You have the power of a healer in the world I created for you. In this world, that power is greater than you imagine. I took that power from you as a girl because I knew you would become a woman who would shame my family's honor, just like Consuelo shamed hers. So I destroyed you, made your body and passion a lifeless shell. Only the power of your mind and the skill of your hands I allowed you to keep."*

"Is that why you took Esteban from me?"

"Yes. He was too much like you, and he was free because he was a man. He wanted to give you a man's freedom. He knew that once you were free you would always choose him over me, and over the gifts of our fathers, our past, our memories. You would take those things and create them again as a gift for him, all for him." Then, losing his self-assurance, his voice lowered to a near whisper. *"Forgive us, m'hija, we — your mother and I — we were afraid"*

I watch the shadows behind the curtain.

"Papá, give me back my secrets of healing."

I am certain that he holds the Ritual of Restoration in

his prison. He tries to respond, but his words now distort as they pass through the curtain.

I run to the next grave, certain that that is where I will find the key to my parents' release from their prison. I look into the grave. Consuelo and her son lie in each other's arms, preserved in eternal youth with the roses of their beloved ones strewn on their motionless bodies. In Consuelo's dead memory is the key to my parents' release, which in turn will restore my ancient knowledge of the Ritual of Restoration. I remember the candy maker. I must have the figurines in the coffin.

The landscape reappears before me in a gigantic scroll: the unknown constellations, the stars and planets of our night sky, the deep blue that signals the end of day, the timeless desert, and finally, the Arabic-Hispanic city. In the tunnel of vendors I find the candy maker waiting for me. I buy the candy.

"Eat it," he says, *"then return to your dead."*

I eat the candy, and the candy maker points me to another exit.

I exit the tunnels, wanting to find the cemetery, but the streets have changed. The buildings, the old colonial houses have huddled together. They block my passage. The streets become narrow walkways, like those in Guanajuato, but hotter, the air bitter; a metallic noise is forming, emerging. I walk into a dark walkway. When I get to the other side, I find myself in the city of Los Angeles. And the smell of impending death calls me. *"Come, Doctor Magdalena, conqueror of death. This way. Defeat me, if you dare."*

"Healer,"
says La Muerte,
"Defeat me and
create me into a
life"

Chapter Five

Los Angeles

"Saint Jude, pray for me and for all who invoke thy aid."

Before an open window, a woman prays to the patron saint of lost causes. I stop and listen to her prayer. *"Come to my assistance at this hour of my great need."*

"Amen," I say. I join her in her beleaguered quest, for I, too, have my quest of lost causes. The sound of automobiles consumes the air, the heat sticks to my skin and creates its own perspiration. I am in Boyle Heights, once a neighborhood of middle class Jews, now a Mexican barrio. It is a place that has been transformed back into that Mexican dream, the colors of an Indian imagination, the gardens of women remembered only in blood with perfumes that insist on existing in this hallucination of concrete. I catch an aroma. A plant: Reyna de la Noche. Its huge white flowers are the seducers of the most beautiful moths that fatalistically dare to search for

flowers in this cement city. And I, as if also a fated creature, follow the fragrance. I am led to the entrance of a garden that only a woman's imagination could create: flowers to accompany the night, and flowers to greet the sun. I recognize the garden. It is Tía Esperanza's, its flowers in a war against time, preserving her memory.

I enter through the gate and wander about this creation of desire. I look towards the house, try to decipher the light emerging from the windows, a malevolence contained, horrible violence. I am filled with fear for the first time since my memory was removed. I hear Tío Pancho's voice, slurred and vulgar. I cannot make out the words but I can hear their insult, their poison. I come closer, to the front door and listen. My cousin Rey, Consuelo's half-brother, is crying with the tearful indignation of someone who has been humiliated by his father.

"Bastard, son of a bitch, son of your whore mother." The old man's words cut through his son's young flesh, still a boy, barely nineteen, still needing a father's love.

"You made me, Francisco. You are my father. Don't treat me like this. Please."

"I'll treat you any way I want in my house. I never asked for nothing. I've got my true son."

"Papá, Frank is dead. Rey is your only son now." Consuelo's voice freezes my blood. It has the cold smell of an

operating room just before death enters and swallows the air.

I open the door, it is unlocked, a past reality altered. The old man always locked his door, always fearful that someone would repay his malice, or that an unpaid gambling debt would find its way to him.

I am blinded by the light, and I can hear only the confused shouts, Rey's cries of despair, Consuelo's unheard pleas, Tío Pancho's barrage of insults. My eyes adjust to the light as Rey takes out a gun. He fires towards his father in the vengeance of a violation of his mother and all the mothers since the arrival of our fathers from the eastern horizon, the reborn Indian prince who has escaped subjugation in the blood of his many regenerations. Desperately, Consuelo throws herself in front of her father, sacrifices herself as I was never willing, an instinct so terrible that she forgets the son inside of her. The bullet tears through her body, but I know that she is not dead. Tío Pancho screams at his violation, his flesh mutilated, he cradles his child, a madness paralyzes him, and he believes that his embrace will save her and defeat Rey, who is also bewildered by the grief of a misguided assassin.

Rey looks at me. *"Doctor Magdalena,"* he shouts, *"save my sister! You've got power over death."*

I run outside to my car. My car. I know it will be

there as if I had arrived in Los Angeles by car and not through the dark alleyways, as if my entry has changed time and its events. The keys are in my jacket. I open the car door and take out my medical bag. But, before I leave, I call an ambulance from my car phone because I realize now that Rey and Tío Francisco did not call until Consuelo was dead. They had grieved over her dying body, not thinking that they could save her. But I can save her. My mind goes into a trance as it does before I go into surgery. It is a sleep of artfulness. My emotions suspend themselves above my head. I can think so clearly that I can see the distant planets and name their hills and rivers of blue gases. My body dissolves itself into the spaces between my molecules. I have become the supreme artist, the great healer. My colleagues have always wondered how I can become so skilled when I am so utterly detached. They envy me because they think it is something to be learned from books. But it is only something to be learned within the imagination.

I re-enter the room that has now become a translucent dream. I see the distorted faces of Rey and Tío Francisco, their cries but muted echoes. My hands touch my cousin's still warm body, her blood struggling to stay alive, the life within her crying at its impending death. My hands, aware of their magic, begin to ward off death. The bleeding slows and in the distance a siren approaches. That was it. I remember that event as it happened: she bled to death. The child inside begins to struggle. The others are surrounding me. They are the ambulance people. *"I'm a doctor,"* I say and they obey me as if I were a god and, for the moment, I am defeating the god of night. I cut Consuelo's clothes, then I make an incision across her belly. I move ever so carefully, as if I am creating a work of art. The waters of life burst upon me, and blood spills forth as I lift the child, tiny and desperate for something more than ancient memory. Someone takes the child as I begin to close the body of my beloved cousin.

I awake from my trance and hear the cries of astonishment coming from the paramedics. Then I fall back into my trance because it has not ended yet, this altered time, I must not lose my magic. I feel drunk, unreal, as if I were the object of an outside ritual, an outside force, desire, an imagination in the realms of death. I experience a masculine confidence in my female powers of healing.

We ride in the ambulance and I watch this vision of the city world unfold before me, a city created by the dreams of men who would conquer not only a land, but an imagination, the desires of the most secret dreams of women and Indians. I imagine what my Spanish forefathers must have thought and wondered as they first looked upon the city of gold, Tenochtitlan. I, too, am a conqueror. I am their child. I have conquered the rivers of time with my desires. I can return to their conquered land and right the masculine wrongs: the rejection of the father of his children, and the sacrifice of the young woman, the virgin-whore, the mother of a new race. I have conquered my ancient fathers who denied to their bastard offspring their memory of the Indians. I have reclaimed the ancient dream, the invisible world of our Indian blood and its secrets about death and time. The swirling colors of the city lights and the color of the blood-stained sky form an answer: they are the same colors worn by the Indians in Mexico City, they speak a language in the light of the memories relegated to the night of our consciousness. What a forbidden secret! The fathers did not want us to know the secrets of the night for fear that we would undo their work, their conquests, their cities in the rivers of time, send them back and thus, prevent our own birth.

They did not trust their mixed-blood children, fearing that the knowledge of their mothers would deny them — the fathers — and their dreams and conquest. So they tried to destroy the memory of our Indian mothers, their world. But their world lived on within the silence of the imagination, in the secret artistry of our hands. I have reconquered the lost dream and I have defeated death and time.

The ambulance stops. They take Consuelo inside and ignore me as I begin to fade in their reality. They are convinced that they have saved my cousin. It is becoming as if I were never there. There is an alley across the street. I cross and enter it. I hear the sounds of a mercado world around the corner of the building. I re-enter the Arabic-Hispanic city. Immediately, the blind pick up the scent of life on my clothes and hands. *"You have defeated death,"* an old blind man cries out in front of a church. I walk past the blind musician boy as he begins to play his guitar and sing a bolero. An old woman, also blind, comes near and finds me by my scent.

"Bless me, temptress of the saints," she says, her head bowed.

I bless her.

I have defeated death with my father's dream, his desire to make me into a great doctor That was my father's making. He defied his culture: I was a girl and he selected me to continue his line, not a genealogy of blood and name, but of imagination and power. He gave me life, and with his life-force came his skill and his arrogance. He conquered tradition, the genealogy of males, made me, a female, in his true image. He made me a conqueror, a woman with her destiny independent of the traditions he espouses. He betrayed his traditions so they could survive in my memory, so that I could create myself anew from all that he was and his fathers were. He gave the world back to a woman when our forefathers took it away from them. I, temptress, destroyer of the jealous saints and violators, our fathers — I have conquered you so that you may live. Padre querido, now I understand you. You love the right thing the wrong way. Now I must free you and the woman you loved, the woman you never humiliated, the woman whose mas-

culine arrogance and lust for power was greater than yours.

I go to the house at the edge of the desert, between two ancient mercados and two times, to where La Doña and Manuela are waiting for me. I am seized by a fatigue of sleepiness that, nevertheless, keeps me awake. I no longer know if I am hallucinating within this mirage, this wonderful reality of desires and of altered time. La Doña and Manuela take me and begin to undress me. They set aside my soiled clothes and I am led to a tin tub where they begin to wash the blood and amniotic fluids off of my skin.

"I am so tired, Doña," I say as my body begins to dissolve into the fluids of sleep.

"You must not sleep, hija," says La Doña. *"Your dead await you. Their time has come. You must go to them or they will be lost in their damnation. They will carry their last secrets, those they deprived you of, with them. You cannot complete the Ritual of Restoration without their withheld secrets."*

La Doña and Manuela dress me. *"You must go before the arrival of the morning."* I look out of the window. The sky is a light ash gray. The white sun pushes its way into the warm night. I take the water jug from the table and empty it in the yard. I fill it with the waters used to wash me. Yes, that is it. I must take the waters of life, life restored by the masculine magic of my father's imagination and the secrets of ancient women. I cross the desert, outracing time again, until I reach the burial grounds of my people. I re-enter the solitary cemetery, its wind-blown oblivion, its decay of sins that even death cannot forget. I look at Consuelo's grave. It is open, and empty. It awaits another of the blood of Valencia, but it will not be my cousin. I have restored her in the rivers of time. Then I walk towards my parents' grave. The sky begins to lighten and I pour the waters of life into my parents' grave, where the roaring of fire and wild animals are heard. I hear the water drop as a rock in a well, the fire roars, explodes out of the grave and forms a curtain of flames. The sun bursts over the mountains and my heart fills with despair. Perhaps I am too late....

"Padres mios, I forgive your excessive love, your diseased hopes."

Perhaps all has failed, perhaps I will awake in the American city of glass with this unfulfilled journey dissolving into the asphalt. And nothing will have been changed. My memories will be returned to me unredeemed, my cousin dead, and a man I still love will continue to dream that I alter his fate.

The force of the sun splits the curtain of flames. Another landscape reveals itself on the other side, another time that accelerates before my eyes. In the distances I see a port of rotting wooden piers, large ships, men in another century's clothes. I hear a horse as it gallops down the docks and, instinctively, I step back. A horse and its rider, a Spanish caballero, emerge in the world of wooden ships. The rider and horse come towards me in full gallop. They break through and into the desert. The caballero rears the horse before me and dismounts. He speaks to me in a language of dreams, a language of colors rather than sounds. He takes out a small leather sack and holds it in one hand, outstretching the other. As I put my hand in his, he tosses the bag at my feet. He does not release my hand. Instead, he takes out a knife and passes it before my eyes, then before his eyes, black and gentle. He turns the knife and makes a small and soft incision on the palm of my hand. It is more an act of love than a violation. The blood wells up in my hand and he bends, presses his mouth and drinks the blood. He stands erect, looks at me, bows ceremoniously and thanks me in his musical language of dreams. Remounting, he and his horse rush wildly back to the port of the wooden ships. Behind him, the curtain of flames closes and extinguishes itself, revealing my parents' common grave, now closed, a marble headstone with the Biblical inscription, "For He loved the world so much that He gave His only begotten child."

I lift the bag and look inside. There, I find burned bones, the remains of my parents. I look at the desert. The sun has arrived and I have saved the condemned souls of my father and mother. Exiting the cemetery, I walk towards the ancient city and enter the Spanish sector. This morning, its old facades seem happy. Walking by the plaza with the kiosk, a band of musicians plays a love song that my grandfather loved.

I invoke the memory of my father and mother, of the young medical student and his beloved as they meet secretly in Chapultepec Park, drink each other's dreams, and leave behind the odor of desire for the trees to breathe. My father loved only one woman. He never had another. He gave her his manhood and she gave him the dreams of her conquistador fathers. Her stories and memories became so real to him that he forgot it was she who visited that Hispanic world in the imagination of her dreams. Yet, in his hands, he held the magic of the Indian curanderos. I, the healer, inherited the secret knowledge of the Indians from my father. He was half Mixtec Indian, a fact that had been long forgotten, our blood so mixed that we suffer forgetfulness of genealogy, we who prefer to look at metal statues of Indians and Spaniards, calling them the fathers instead of remembering through our blood. I stop by the kiosk and listen to the rest of the song.

I wonder — how could a man and a woman, who understood the love between them so well, deny their daughter the same secrets. I obeyed them in all things. I even left Esteban and went away to school. What they destroyed in me remains hidden. I never told them that I loved Esteban, and that he had been left alone to defend his love for me. After a while, he only imagined that I had loved him, for I had given him nothing, not even a few personal words written in secret. Even then I knew that if he could prove that I still loved him, he would find me and force me to choose between my father's dream and my desires.

My father always said that a man like that was irresponsible. *"You are better off without him, hija. You'll find a respectable man to love you. Some day, you will. But this man is worthless."*

Not to me! I would have followed him to the end of his dreams. My father knew that. And I forced myself not to think of Esteban. I had inflicted a forgetfulness upon my heart. La Doña was right. Forgetfulness was my greatest desire. Until now.

I want my memories back, but not disjointed and episodic as they have been. I want the restoration of my soul with memory. I must ask La Doña.... God....! La Doña awaits me. The hour of her death has arrived.

Chapter Six

The Restoration

As I run through the city and the mercado, I am dreaming that I am falling through a cloud. Then I am being transported to a land of red soil, the land from which my people sprang forth and worshiped the old gods of the caves and trees. I dream that I am in a forest of young trees with branches that intertwine to form a prison. But I command the road to open before me. At the center of the forest is a figure masked as death. *"Soy La Muerte,"* says the masked figure. I go and rip the mask off, afraid it will be me, my mirror self in the city of glass, a woman who preferred to kill genealogies within her womb rather than bring life to the light. But it is not my face that is revealed. It is a naked skull. It is so alone that I pity its hollow sockets that have been deprived of tears.

"Muerte," I say. *"I am a Dreamer and the Healer."*

"Healer," says La Muerte. *"Give me life. They sing of*

miracles in the mercado, and that you have the power of death. Defeat me and create me into a life."

"No, Muerte, you are unhappy because of the burden of the sinners. I shall send you my dead, cleansed of their sins. They will bring you joy during the eternal night."

La Muerte begins to wail. *"You have taken the young woman, your cousin, from the House of Death. I have fallen in love with her. I can never be happy, Healer."*

"She is the eternal woman, Muerte. She will never enter the land of the dead again. A soul taken from Death can never be reclaimed by you. When she has outlived her life in the world of glass and machines, she will join the women of the lost tribe of the mercado world. With them, she will wait to be reborn into another generation."

"Healer," says La Muerte, *"let me look upon the face of the eternal woman once a year. Command a price for the relief of my sorrow."*

I ask La Muerte to give me the secret Song of Restoration, the chant of life and death, and, in return, I will give him the power to become a man once a year, on Saint Jude's festival day. On that night, he can search for my cousin in time's rivers and have one look at her before returning to the kingdom of night.

La Muerte whispers a song in my ear, and I awake

from my dream as I reach the house of La Doña del Olvido.

La Doña is dying as she lies on her bed. At her side, Manuela's tears rise from the deepest wells of her being. From deep within the center of her soul, her tears form in eternal love, then silently flow down her cheeks.

"Healer," whispers Manuela. *"Restore my comadre. Even now, Death has his hand on her."*

I go into the kitchen area and start a fire on the large adobe fireplace. I, a woman who fears fire because it killed my flesh — my life-givers — now commands the flames. I take the clothes soaked with the waters of life, the amniotic fluids and blood of my cousin and put them in the fire as I begin to sing the Song of Restoration.

From the flames of strife

All life arises.

Then, I empty the bag of bones into the flames. The fire turns blue, changing from flame to a suspended liquid. I continue the song.

The earth remembers her beginnings

And awaits the gifts of the healers.

The gifts of life and the desires of night.

The Sun remembers his beginning and his

conquest of the

Eternal night.

All gods must be remembered, all life loved,

all offspring

Traitors and lovers of memories.

Gods of night, Gods of light, cease your strife

and celebrate,

For the world is being born.

I take a jar and pass it through the blue liquid flames that do not burn. Returning to La Doña's side, I slowly pour the liquid through her lips.

"Drink, Doña," says Manuela. *"The healer has found the cure for our affliction."*

La Doña swallows and is engulfed in a blinding blue

light. Manuela and I are forced to turn away from the fierce light. It surrounds La Doña as she stands before us. Suddenly, she begins to drop the vestiges of old age, like leaves. She becomes unsheathed, layer after layer of eternity melts before our eyes. At last, she emerges from the blue light, a young woman, as pure and uncontaminated as the priestess of Teotihuacan before the end of the Toltec universe.

Manuela now looks at me. Her time has come. I give her the liquid of blue flames and repeat the chant. She, too, is engulfed by blue flames and emerges a young woman.

I return to the fireplace and the fire of blue liquid is now dying. Once more I dip the jar into the flames, for I owe one more beloved of mine an altered fate.

La Doña and Manuela enter the kitchen area.

"Magdalena," says La Doña. *"We must remove your memory of this place, along with its secrets, and reunite you with the woman who sleeps in the city of glass. We will return you now, complete with your wisdom of healing."*

"And the memories of my family — my past?"

"We can remove those as well, or restore them to you when you return. You must choose. What shall it be, temptress of the saints? Olvido o recuerdos?"

"I choose memory, Doña."

"You are a wise woman, for without the memories of our fathers we cannot find the secrets of our darkness."

"Doña," I say, stopping her as she begins to mix the herbs of forgetfulness. *"Let me remain one more night. Please."*

"You must return!" says Manuela, a note of urgency in her voice. *"You are still of the world of glass and machines."*

"No!" I retort. *"In a dream, you created a portal of lace. You must return me there, tonight, before you free me from this world!"*

That night, before I slept, las brujas prepared themselves to eat my dreams for a last time. I took the water of blue flames and mixed it with the clay that Esteban had given me. Methodically, I began to sculpt the clay into the figure of a heart with eyes. Then I begin to dream. But I can only remember the dreams for less than a second, for the brujas are consuming them. They are fulfilling the spell of forgetfulness as I spin through the portal of lace and meet my loved ones, living and dead, only to quickly forget the words we speak to each other. I am dreaming of Mexico City. I am dreaming of my grandmother's house. I am dreaming of Tía Esperanza growing her flowers from another galaxy. I am dreaming that Consuelo has become a moon and then changes herself into a purple planet. I am dreaming that Esteban becomes a boy as he grows older and begins his life again... I am dreaming . . . I am dreaming . . . I am . . . I am Magdalena Ibarra.

"M'hija," my father's voice returns from the dead. *"I live within you, the memories of your antepasados."*

I dream of the conquistadores and they worship a native god of feathers . . . I dream....

"The dreamers dream of the origins of life from distant galaxies, a metamorphosis of color, that ventured forth into the fate of men while the gods were creating and re-creating the world five times."

Chapter Seven

Coda:

The Storyteller

In the villages outside the rising cities of modern Mexico, and in the Hispanic corridors of the ancient urbanized centers, the whispers and rumors remain untouched by modernity, by technology and the currently fashionable skepticism. Few appear to care that all things cease to exist when they are forgotten, such as the gods and the events of older days, events that are now deemed too fantastic simply because the oft-quoted science of the modern world has not yet discovered the secrets of the origins of submatter and the eternal movements of energy.

But in the villages and urban corridors, the whispers are remembered in the secret dreams that seize the dreamer in fits of sweat and commotion.

The dreamers dream of the origins of life from distant galaxies, a metamorphosis of color, one that ventured forth into the fate of men while the gods were creating and re-creating the world five times.

The stories are told to children in the shadows of night and sung in the boleros of the old men and the young boys. People tell of a woman who weeps for her children at night, whose wailing laments are heard in the air above the streets or by the rivers or by the sea. Midnight lovers, when walking by the church, hear an old man who has been condemned to sweep the churches throughout eternity. It is his fate for having killed his daughter because she exchanged a kiss with her beloved.

On the Festival of Saint Jude, patron saint of lost causes, a few days before the Day of the Dead, the villagers and the urban dwellers are said to have seen a young man who repeatedly searches the mercados. He searches for a young woman. The people say that she is a beautiful bruja, and that the young man is La Muerte. He is condemned never to find his beloved, for if he did, death would be no more and the world would be destroyed because it is the gods who have reserved immortality for themselves.

In the mercados there are merchants who sell the secrets of desire: love, sleep, and forgetfulness. But these paths in the mercados are secret and one must be careful for what one wishes lest he find himself buying his own deepest desires.

It is sung in the cafes and cantinas that a woman asked a bruja to remove her memory and soul, and that the bruja sent an apparition of the woman to our common world. But the bruja kept the woman's soul until she learned a secret from her existential prison.

The city dwellers, recipients of the soft and persistent winds created by the voices of humans, have heard that Hernan Cortés weeps as he rides his horse through the streets on each anniversary of La Noche Triste. Cortés's weeping, however, is a lament for his own betrayal by his king, his loss of his conquered kingdom, while his two sons of his two wives, both sons named Martín, follow him steadfastly with swords drawn at the ready, both determined to protect the honor of their father through the eternal night of death.

These, and many more similar occurrences remain hidden in the courtyards of the old village churches or, they remain concealed in the secret tunnels of unearthed pyramids, or in the enclosed cobbled streets of the Hispanic cities throughout Mexico.

The Illustrations

Design from flat stamp found in Azcapotzalco, D.F. Now in National Museum of Mexico

Symbol of a constellation, or the sceptre of Quetzalcoatl. Found in Guerrero, Mexico

Cylindrical stamp. Place of the dead. Found in Mexico City

Flat stamp showing human hand (Maitl), from Texcoco

The earth in bloom. Stamp found in Mexico City

The Illustrations

Cover, page 5, page 66

Mictlantecuhtli, lord of the dead; Custodian of the bones of all past human generations; ceramic; from Tierra Blanca, Veracruz; Totonac: A.D. 600-900. Museo de Antropología de la Universidad Veracruzana, Jalapa, Veracruz, Mexico

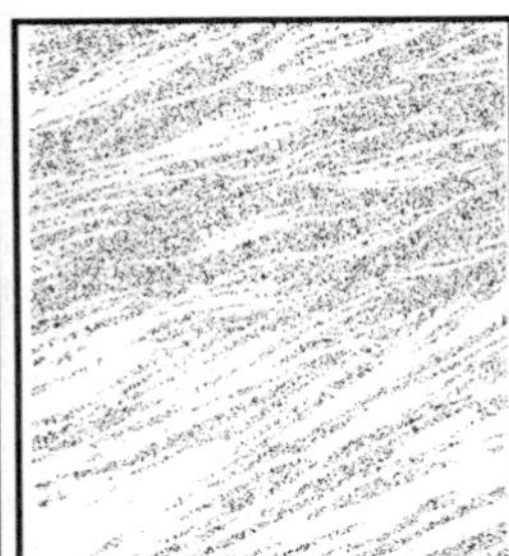

Pages 6-7, page 86

Flames, adapted from *Muerte en Chinameca,* The Assassination of Emiliano Zapata: 1919: Woodcut, Salvador Romero

Page 8

Adapted from sculpture, Francisco Villa on Horseback, Mexico City

Page 32

Bronze portrait of Maximilian; sculpture; Felipe Soto; 1864 Museo Nacional de Historia, Chapultepec Castle, Mexico City